D1523883

Casanova in Venice

Casanova in Venice

A RAUNCHY RHYME

Kildare Dobbs

Nine Original Wood Engravings
by Wesley W. Bates

The Porcupine's Quill

Library and Archives Canada Cataloguing in Publication

Dobbs, Kildare, 1923–
    Casanova in Venice : a raunchy rhyme / Kildare Dobbs.

ISBN 978-0-88984-332-5

    I. Bates, Wesley W. II. Title.

PS8507.035C373 2010   C811'.54   C2010-903542-9

Published by The Porcupine's Quill, 68 Main Street,
PO Box 160, Erin, Ontario NOB 1T0.

Readied for the press by Wayne Clifford.

Represented in Canada by the Literary Press Group.
Trade orders are available from University of Toronto Press.

We acknowledge the support of the Ontario Arts Council, the Canada
Council for the Arts, the Government of Canada through the Canada
Book Fund and the Ontario Media Development Corporation for our
publishing programme.

To Jonathan Williams

A periphrastic study in a worn-out poetical fashion.
           – T.S. Eliot

Entwine our arts with laughters low.
           – James Joyce

Preface

Readers of poetry in English have most often felt at ease with a tradition that found rich expression in anthologies like *The Oxford Book of English Verse* edited by the late Sir Arthur Quiller-Couch, a tradition that inclined strongly to lyric, elegiac and even sentimental poetry. The comic, mock-heroic and satirical genres were out. Works like Samuel Butler's *Hudibras* (C17th) and Jonathan Swift's sarcastic poems and satires were ignored, though not because they were written in rhyming octosyllabic couplets. For this metre is used by Milton in 'Il Penseroso' and 'L'Allegro', by Henry King in his 'Exequy' and by Andrew Marvell in his finest lyrics. But with its galloping rhythm and the neat smack of its rhymes, the measure is ideally suited to satire, invective and wit; and no less, perhaps, to lying and persuasion. (Remember: 'The truest poetry is the most feigning'.)

Contemporary poetry, especially in North America, tends to be in free verse. That is, it takes a form in which the words are arranged on the page to *look* like metrical verse. This makes it more difficult to succeed at, except for the rare poets with well-tuned ears. Unluckily, free verse is also vulnerable to fraud. Since my subject is very much an eighteenth-century figure, I decided to try my hand at those rhyming couplets, and to use some of the classical machinery and conventions that Casanova might have used. Hence the occasional reappearance of nymphs, gods and goddesses, the lyre, and the Muses.

The narrative frame is based loosely on Casanova's *Mémoires*, a brilliant work which everyone should read. Each poem in the following sequence is headed by an epigraph quoted from that work in Arthur Machen's translation, unless some other author is indicated. The poem leaves the hero astride the roof of the Doge's palace, at the beginning of his famous escape from the Leads, i.e., the cells under the roof, to which the State Inquisition had consigned him.

Giacomo Casanova

Economy in pleasure is not to my taste.

Awake, my lute! and trumpets blow
for one who never could say no!
so powerful his virile charm
a wench would catch him by the arm
and pull him down to kiss and fondle her
in the seclusion of a gondola.
This was a man so much traduced –
though less seducer than seduced –
called monster of Venetian lust
for whom good Christians had disgust.
Of all his scolds himself the worst
since in old age he'd boast and curse,
accuse himself, though not to blame
for playing Nature's sweetest game
with naughty females after dinner.
God hates the sin but loves the sinner,
he told himself, so seized the day,
or rather night, and sinned away
and thus assured of heavenly love
delighted in each raunchy move.
The flame of amorous desire
flares briefly like a straw-fed fire
and just as briefly flickers out.
We wonder, *What was that about?*
Why did we sigh and lose our sleep
and hold our dignity so cheap?
For certain, every nubile dame
rolled in the sack is much the same.
Often our man was set to wed
but freedom was his choice instead.
It's fine to have a loving wife –
but penile servitude for life?

No way! But more, it would be rash
to keep a woman without cash.
For he too often lacked the ready –

Poet, wait up a moment, steady!
Whom do we speak of? Name the man,
describe his person if you can.

Time has pronounced him lovers' king,
at board and bed the hottest thing
whose charm no female could resist –
onto her back as soon as kissed!
Con artist first of all the crew,
both *con* in French and English too.
He would be handsome, said a peer,
were he not ugly, and we hear
smallpox had scarred his cheeks along;
complexion sallow; features strong;
in person very tough and wiry,
in temperament vengeful and fiery.
Called vain – the accusation's phony
for what he was, was Macaroni.
He wore such clothes as would assure a
repute for *la bella figura*,
moreover those who called him vain
had no idea of his brain.
Opulent people almost never
believe a semi-pauper clever.
If you're so smart, sneers Mistress Bitch,
(through golden teeth) how come not rich?

I have to interrupt once more,
give us the name, I must implore!
Maybe we know him, maybe not,
but please don't put us on the spot.

Be straight with us and play the game –
all we're demanding is the name.

His Christian names, if you must know,
were Giacomo Hieronimo,
his last – I've worked the subject over
but can't find rhymes for Casanova.
except the cockney one displayed –
and I'm not cockney, I'm afraid.
New House, it means, this patronymic,
some joker must have found this gimmick,
as if he said, Heigh ho! my nasty
nature can institute a dynasty.

Zanetta

A perfect beauty, sixteen years of age.

The boy's young mother's fresh and pretty
but she withholds the milk of pity.
Love is a passion deep and warm.
basic in the maternal form,
and this she shows for all to see
on stage, though not for family.
Zanetta's a comedienne
who acts her finest part for men,
to London goes when fortune beckons
into the bed of George the Second,
leaving the sickly little lad
loveless in Venice, lost and sad.

Grimm truths

And don't you remember the babes in the wood?
— Brothers Grimm

Dark are the dreams of lads and maids
who wander in benighted shades
and dark the hut where hungry urchin
goes seeking candy, cakes, and searching
for sweetness lacking in his menu
only to find the witch's venue.
And now the lonely child is lost,
his life for candy is the cost.
Babe in the woods is still the tale.
The child sits down and starts to wail —

Mother, don't do this to me, please,
Oh if you love me, on my knees!
don't leave me in a world so wild,
Mother, I'm just a little child!

Now this

Venice is a city rich in gold but richer still in beauty.
                                        – Petrarch

Consider now the place and time,
the age of reason, faith and doubt,
imperial Venice past its prime
whose laden vessels still sail out

to carry all her shrinking trade,
upon the wide indifferent sea
in which she sinks, her stones decayed,
her cellars crumbling secretly;

yet on the drifting waters still
the image of her glory lies,
illusions being her fatal skill,
quicksilvered glass reflects her skies

and from her palaces and towers
echoes return of song and bell
in disputation of the hours
(what o'clock, only time can tell).

On which side of the looking-glass
did the young mother act her play?
and did the boy, deluded, pass
the barrier? Or did he stay?

Life is a comedy

I had at that time reached the age of eight years.

Giacomo claims he can't recall
his first eight years of life at all,
and yet his family was party
to the *commedia dell' arte.*

Hearing the stories every day,
he must have thought to live that way
with cheating wives and scheming grifters
at play with parasites and drifters,
and complicated love affairs
involving many amorous pairs,
masks and disguises, often cruel
swindles and pranks – and then a duel.

These stories from the lively stage
inspire his memoirs in old age.
His mother as his *Columbine*
for *Harlequin* would sigh and pine
and trick that nasty old buffoon
the grasping miser *Pantaloon*
out of his money. And meanwhile
the *Captain* twirls mustachios while
he exercises all his wits
just for one glimpse of mama's tits!

With mother gone now, in her place is
a plethora of pretty faces
and these in many different ways
will be his loves through all his days.
But now, the sickly little fellow
is pestering old *Pulcinello*
to tell him where his mother went –
what country in which continent.

He dreams of following her track
doing his best to bring her back.

The boy had nosebleeds, but his nose,
though long, was shorter far than those
worn on their masks by *i dottori*
grotesques! – but that's another story.
And strange to tell, the boy's condition
was cured, though not by a physician,
and, odder yet, the treatment which
prevailed was given by a witch.

Consolation

In this way did my family get rid of me.

The cure for pain must surely be
a warm dose of felicity,
which can exist in double kind,
pleasure of body and of mind.
Giacomo sought to quench his yearning
by giving all his mind to learning.
Doctors had ordered change of air –
to Padua they sent him where
under a young priest's kindly rule
at Dr Pozzi's boarding-school,
the boy grew stronger every week
while learning Latin, maths and Greek;
and to distract from carnal sin
took lessons on the violin.

There was another source of joy
that comforted the growing boy,
his new-discovered inner sense
of personal intelligence.
As bright wind along Alpine paths,
the lucid certainties of maths,
pleasure to cure the heart's dull pain,
bring order to a troubled brain.
The classic words of antique sages
express the wisdom of the ages,
imparting, though at second hand,
experience he can understand.
So now with sharpened faculties
the student looks on life with ease.

As he grows taller every day,
testosterone comes into play
and through his arteries and veins
is gushing like the April rains.

In lurid dreams it intimates
vague notions how to please bedmates.
The priest's young sister at thirteen
is paid to keep Giacomo clean.
to wash his hands, his neck, his chest
and dutifully all the rest;
and one day, rubbing at his thigh,
allows her hand to stray too high,
which stimulates his not-to-mention
(she *vows* it wasn't her intention)
to rise, embarrassing the youth,
who thinks this quick response uncouth.

Bettina (that's the wench's name)
is far from feeling quite the same,
but both draw back from passion's brink,
(and they are wise to stop and think).
From virtue Tina's had a lapse,
she entertains three other chaps.
In danger of being caught with three men,
she feigns possession by a demon,
yells loudly with convulsive twists
so that they call the exorcists.
They bring a hairy Capuchin,
who tells the fiend to cease his din,
making him masculine, please note,
nor giving him a petticoat.

The damsel calls the friar a stinker,
an imbecile and brandy drinker.
It seems he doesn't even know
demons are always spirits, so
have neither height nor weight nor sex
like angels, they're pure intellects.
The friar, defeated, does a bunk.
Why, then comes in a handsome monk.

A smooth, well-groomed Dominican,
(the hairy won't come in again)
he orders all spectators out
(and Casanova has no doubt
what this manoeuvre really meant –
the monk and girl on pleasure bent –
and, if the parents knew, would kill 'im).
The monk takes out his aspergillum,

What's that? she cries. *It's holy water –
and now the cure,* he says, *dear daughter!*
And then as over her he bent,
she does not fear the instrument.
Others have seen a pious monk –
Bettina sees a handsome hunk!
Soon she is calm, and with a smile
is safe in Morpheus' arms a while.
Giacomo sighs, for he has guessed
her stratagem and is impressed –
a sadder and a wiser boy –
by her swift and resourceful ploy.
Of all his loves this was the start,
although it lacked the happiest part.
All his affairs will be the same –
more than the goal, he loves the game.

Serene Republic

She looks a sea Cybele. Fresh from Ocean,
Rising with her tiara of proud towers …
— Byron

The splendours of Venetian state
in her decline did not abate
but shone upon the glimmering tide
with domes and towers that rose beside
narrow canals where fell, reflected,
the marble palaces erected
to shed their golden scattered light
and magnify the Doge's might.

Elect of peers, robed in brocade
this prince of oriental trade,
could seldom let his men embark
sans blessings of the Patriarch.
And yearly took his barge to sea
to wed with gorgeous ceremony,
in every circumstance dramatic,
the heaving, fickle Adriatic.

The Patriarch took charge of souls,
sinners he damned to hell's hot coals,
to spend eternal life in pain
proving God's kindliness again.
And for the righteous heavenly bliss,
where men and angels meet and kiss
and play Scarlatti good and loud
and dance with Moses on a cloud.

Discriminating in this mission,
the Doge supported Inquisition
with swarming spies and cruel brutes
who put the questions with their boots.
Thus working for the force of good
Caesar and God as one withstood
the never-sleeping, mad exertions
of those who engineered subversions.

Just a minute

I was foolish enough to write the truth ...

Come, step aside from scene and act
and ask whether these tales be fact:
are old men's memories robust
enough to earn a reader's trust?
Hear what old Hesiod's Muses say
true in the past and true today:
O many a lie like truth we tell –
but true things we declare as well.

And for the tales of Giacomo
we have the word of those who know
his story in those far-off days –
we can trust anything he says
or almost all, since nothing's certain
in this life, but the final curtain.
Himself declared, when at death's door,
Truth is the one god I adore.

The University of Bo, Padua

*A meadow without grass, a saint without a name
and café without doors.* (Proverb)

Still in pursuit of solid knowledge,
Giacomo finds his way to college
and at the 'Varsity of Bo
(means Ox.) learns all there is to know
of law, both civil law and canon,
and other things we find a man in –
as drinking, gambling, fighting, fencing,
and further enterprise in wenching.

Feeling his clothes are rather shabby,
he dons the cassock of an abbé –
that is, takes minor orders in
the lowest clergy, to begin
the church career by grandma planned.
Now at eighteen he seems so grand,
well-armed, she thinks, against adversity
as doctor of law, by the university.

But,
mistress, wife, *job* – each is a trap
for such a lively, restless chap,
and luckily there's a solution,
an ancient Roman institution:
Patron and client's a relation
persisting in the Italian nation
by which much talent finds support,
with honour to the richer sort,
and all his life our hero'll find
generous patrons of the kind.

(Envious scholars have no right
to call our man a parasite,
since they themselves are quite well off
by feeding at the public trough.)

Giacomo, more than any man,
enjoys the gifts of charlatan
so useful to a man of parts
when practising the learned arts
of medical practitioner or lawyer
where quackery's a blessing for you.
Medicine was his dream, indeed,
and many times he did succeed
in making cures – unqualified,
yet none of all his patients died.

At Padua law lectures were
held in a hall which used to share
with physic lectures held next door
a wide connecting corridor.
Here when the students got together,
discussing everything but weather,
Giacomo caught essential gnosis
of doctoring by sheer osmosis.

Pheromones

The chief business of my life has always been to indulge my senses.

I.

Come all you scolds with tight-arsed biases
who charge this man with satyriasis
and make an envious to-do
because he's getting more than you,
consider first his race and times
for blood was hot in warmer climes
and pretty females danced and tripped
but seldom in a hot tub laved
their dewy limbs, nor armpits shaved,
yet still smelt fragrant when they stripped.
unlike the women of today
whose pheromones are washed away
by lathered soap till squeaky clean
all in the name of sound hygiene.
Sterile at last, their cleanness such,
the message is Just look, don't touch.

Amid real scents the young man strayed
that roused for fight his ready blade –
so the proud war-horse pricks his ears
and snuffs the breeze: from far he hears
the trumpet call to charge and do
whatever Nature tells him to.
Thus sleepy firemen wake alert,
slide down the pole, throw on a shirt
with other clothes, and race away
to fight the first fire of the day;
so Casanova at first sniff
is ready for the nearest quiff.

2.

But don't imagine for a minute
that female scents are all that's in it.
Giacomo's redolent as well
with an attractively male smell.
He washes well and shaves his cheek
and changes stockings once a week
but nothing masks the pheromone
special to Giacomo alone.
Two nuns a hundred yards away:
one whiff – they're in the family way;
the Virgin's statue bumps and grinds
and *putti*, wiggling fat behinds,
when this young fellow passes near
stick fingers in the prelate's ... ear.
The orphans in Vivaldi's care
sensing Giacomo from the air
break into song and scrape their fiddles
in all the hot hey-diddle-diddles.
Two spirits, coming by this way,
materialize and goose a gay,
and doggies, well-informed by nose,
stop sniffing to play tippy-toes.

3.

Don't scold the girls, don't curse the man
for having all the fun they can.
Oh, no one should distribute blame
When Holy Nature plays her game.
Let not her sweetness turn to sour
when pheromones exert their power.

Pantaloon

I have always been fond of highly seasoned, rich dishes.

Say, poet, what is this you tell me –
you like your women warm and smelly,
their armpits and their legs unshaved?
Some folks would find these tastes depraved!

And yet the experienced palate favours
whatever of corruption savours –
as cheese and game and some affairs
between the sheets, below the stairs,
or in another kind of fun,
the naughty deed played with a nun.
Giacomo travelled, often slept
in beds and taverns badly kept
with bedbugs swarming in the covers
and fleas attacking sleepy lovers –
and not just fleas but crabs and lice
and other creatures far from nice.
There's kindness in a wench's lap
but also the French pox and clap.
Hearing of these in terms far sweeter,
our man said, *Syphile? Glad to meet her!*
And before long he came to greet
the too familiar spirochaete,
and more than once he felt the burn
of Gonorrhoea in her turn.
All this you know, and I digress
to speak for decent cleanliness.

Peripeteia

The lucky stroke which, taking me from the vile profession
of a fiddler, raised me to the rank of a grandee.

A summer night – the rising moon
casts sequins on the dark lagoon,
squandering her coin in spendthrift measure,
all glittering like imperial treasure –
Venetians jingle in their pockets
an ever-flowing tide of ducats,
but our man, now aged twenty-eight,
is fallen to the dismal state
of playing second fiddle in
a dance-band, where he cannot win
respect or decent livelihood
and scarce enough to buy him food,
yet all around is milk and honey.
This town, he knows, depends on money,
on doubloons, sequins, louis, francs,
bills of exchange, and drafts on banks,
no matter where their lives will range
Venetians know the rates of 'change
to the last soldi, one percent –
our man can barely pay his rent.

His stint was ending when one night
our fiddler, leaving, caught a sight
of an old senator robed in red
who clearly thought it time for bed,
as wearily he made his way
across the empty moonlit quay.

The youth, emerging, had to stop
because he saw the noble drop
a letter as he stepped aboard
his gondola. *Excellency – a word!*
the fiddler cried, then ran to pick up
the letter – taking time to hiccup
– well anyway, a shortish time,
seeing we're reaching for a rhyme –
presented it with graceful bow
to the old senator, who now
thanked him with a most courtly air,
then: *Where do you live? I'll take you there!*

They hadna gone a league, a league but barely half
(this line, snitched from *Sir Patrick Spens*, is offered for a laugh),
when, faint of voice, the senator
calls on the smiling fiddler for
assistance, as quite suddenly
he's paralyzed! and fears that he
is done for! Our man's quick to act
and diagnosing as a fact
a nasty apoplectic stroke,
with all the skill he can invoke
recalls that firstly there's a need
to fetch a surgeon who must bleed
the patient and reduce the pressure,
then a physician for good measure.
Which aid our hero brings at once
(at medicine he's not a dunce).
The learned leech applies a plaster
of mercury, a near-disaster
till Casanova rips away
the noxious thing, and saves the day.
Diet and nature do the rest.
And so all happens for the best.

Then spoke the noble convalescent:
Young friend, you have been ever-present
and never once left my bedside.
Some spirit must have been your guide!
To me you were a wise physician,
though you appeared a mere musician.
Good parts you have for one so young
but such to higher powers belong.

The senator went on and said,
Without your skill I would be dead!
Son, your protectors hitherto
have never given you your due:
instead have tried to make you,
first a very junior abbé,
then lawyer, soldier and a scabby
fiddler at weddings, underpaid,
and yet you were the one whose aid
preserved my life, for which I owe
you everything, as you must know.
I am the one who saw your worth
and now I give you a new birth:
To thank you for your faithful care
I hereby call you son and heir,
my house your home, with bed and board
and privileges of a lord,
servant and gondola at command
and clothes appropriately grand.

For young Giacomo, what a joy!
At last the rank he can enjoy!
With senator for father he
can riot with impunity,
and so at first the lucky pup
does his mad best to live it up.

Now, Casanova works a scam,
possessing what he knows is sham
expertise in magic arts,
and disingenuously imparts
some of his pseudo-occult lore
to his too trusting Senator.
Reason is stilled, cannot resist as
the young mage cites his Trismegistus,
then Paracelsus and the whole
hermetic lore and rigmarole.
In this respect and only this,
(an oracle called *Parelis*)
the man's acuity is flawed
– that Casanova is a fraud
he cannot know or wish to know.
He needs to trust his Giacomo
and is afraid to ask a question;
while his new son can't risk confession.
Bragadino's the noble name
by which the patron won his fame.
In all things, save this superstition,
he is a wise man and logician.

Love of women

My ardent nature, my irresistible love of pleasure,
my unconquerable independence ...

Our man is captured by a countess
whose youthful charms are sweet and bounteous
especially when she sheds her nightie
to sacrifice to Aphrodite
and then to sacrifice again
and after that again, again!
How many times? our hero sighs.
Who's counting, love! the countess cries.
She's young, she's strong, her vigour's boundless,
Giacomo calls her 'Countess Countless'
and loves her truly for her mind
and really exquisite behind
which to behold evokes a pang,
– it's like a beautiful meringue!
As sea assaults Illyrian shores
crashing in surf and foam, and roars
in rage because the rocks withstand
incessant blows, and guard the land
(remembering water's softer than
sweet flesh that can subdue a man),
just so our hero like a rock
is ready for each tender shock.
(But afterwards he needs to keep
his strength up with ten hours of sleep.)
The *Memoirs*, though, are silent when
we need to know what happened then.
The girl fades kindly from the screen
of memory, and then another scene.

Our laws were framed to neuter youth
to shield those longer in the tooth
from all effective competition
in the great market of coition.

Deep shock! – a lovely teacher lays
a tender lad in all the ways
that Eros knows, and new ones too
when she wakes up the teenage zoo.
The boy knows he's in Paradise
and has to tell the other guys.
Result: too many tell the tale,
and teacher takes her hots to jail.

There's nothing that makes matrons rage
more than this difference in age.
Not so in Casanova's time
when naughty girls were in their prime
as early as their fourteenth year.
These are the chits our man holds dear,
with one is so besotted that
he means to marry with the brat!
She's thirteen, he is twenty-nine,
both young, the combination's fine,
but when her daddy hears of it
he's seized with a conniption fit –
whatever that is – bad for sure!
He does his level best to cure
her adolescent lechery
so locks her in a nunnery.
Her lover's plunged in black despair,
since he has no idea where
the convent is in which she frets
enclosed behind the cloistered gates
imprisoned by the convent wall
– if she remembers him at all.

The Nun of Murano

Oh, how sweet they are! those denials of a loving mistress,
who delays the happy moment only for the sake of enjoying
its delights better!

I.

It is the nature of a man
to find such pleasure as he can
and cater to that nature's need
without excess of lust and greed.
It's also, thinking souls believe,
more blest to give than to receive,
and that same gift doubles the bliss
of sweetness in a lover's kiss.

Yet if there's trouble that dismays
most men, it is the maze
of difficulties raised by women
– a sea of deviousness to swim in –
devised to give themselves the air
of triumph in a love-affair.
To lead their lover in a dance
is their idea of true romance.

But Giacomo is not like us
and loves the silly games and fuss
of girls, and everything about them –
there's no way he can do without them.
What if they do blow hot and cold,
now shy and bashful, next time bold?
With a big scene they'll end their play,
increasing pleasure by delay.

So in electrical machines
power's enhanced by devious means,
passing from coil to coil to induce
a step-up in the charge of juice
often by ten times or a score
– with extra coils it can be more.
When a man's lust becomes illicit, he
staggers with surging electricity

that swiftly leaps from groin to brain,
from spark to soup and back again,
enhanced with each synapsis passed,
each voltage higher than the last,
until the charge is strong enough
to land the victim on his duff!
Thus abstinence makes lust grow stronger
until our man can wait no longer.

Then luckily for his affair
no fishwife, whore or slut is near,
no chambermaid or artist's model,
no naughty broads to kiss and cuddle,
since each of Eve's lubricious daughters
is much the same in certain quarters
and can relieve a man as surely
as the sweetheart he loves so purely.

When he's in love our man is chaste,
unless by chance he should be faced
with sudden joys he can't refuse –
or all is lost or still to lose –
or just to keep his gonads warm –
or any port in any storm!
And who can blame him in this plight
for whom all cats are grey at night?

But all is well in the event.
The girl is able to have sent –
no longer any need to guess –
a message giving her address:
a convent on Murano's isle,
locked up with vestals for a while,
where she's sequestered safe from blame
and Catarina is her name.

Now each week on the Sabbath day
young Casanova makes his way
by water to Murano, where
in the nun's church he kneels in prayer,
hears mass and, gawking through the screen,
a grille that rises in between
the nuns and layfolk on their knees,
looks for his lovely little squeeze.

And sometimes he achieves a glimpse
of her among the Vestal nymphs,
from whence she sends a sultry look
that makes him drop his prayer book
and wonder in frustration when
he'll get his jollies once again.
It's one thing briefly to postpone,
another to find himself alone.

There's comes a chilling Sunday when
the girl's not there to sing *Amen*.
Later she sends him word to say
she's somewhat indisposed today.
In fact she's got some gut upheaval –
make that *miscarriage!* – and, worse evil,
she's bleeding with no help from surgeons
and has to hide it from the virgins.

At once resourceful Giacomo
in secret sends, to staunch the flow,
such quantities of laundered linen
under a cloak to take it in
around the person of a fat
old dame, with a distracting hat,
along with a most loving letter
that Catarina soon felt better.

2.

On his next visit there occurs
an incident that quickly stirs
our hero's instinct for adventure –
he's mad for intrigue as the French are:
a woman on the wharf or street
stares at him, throwing at his feet
a letter – then quickly speeds away
before he finds a word to say.

Aboard his gondola he tries
to understand what this implies.
It's a brief letter from a nun
suggesting that they meet for fun;
she's often noticed him at mass,
he's handsome and a gent with class.
He's ready to believe – what's more he's
vain enough to trust her story.

This Mary Magdalene, in truth,
a lovely girl with brains and youth,
assumed the veil to live a life
free of the serfdom of a wife,
to study and indulge her thought
of living as a free soul ought
among great spirits of the mind,
the famous dead and all their kind.

As free in sex as in her learning
she satisfies a certain yearning
as Sappho did with acolytes
and shares her Dionysian rites
with pretty little Catarina,
who from her innocence has been a
willing novice at the game,
while dropping Casanova's name.

She boasts that in his amorous ardour
he's cleverer and stronger, harder,
than any other man she's met.
At which the nun confesses that
she has a fine stud of her own,
a Frenchman too, hard as a bone,
but tells herself it's time she tried
this other fellow on the side.

Our man's excited by the chance
to plunge into a new romance
and with a holy bride this time
from God's extensive and sublime
seraglio or gynaeceum;
no one may touch or even see 'em
unless they're veiled from top to toe
and even then sex is no go.

Think what a thrill it would excite
to spend a most unholy night
cheating the universe's king!
Vengeance for Joseph and the gang
whose girls, by deities annexed,
refused their horny husbands sex!
To love a nun and then to boast
of cuckolding the lord of hosts!

To think like this, you have to be
from brain-washed youth a good R.C.
You'd have to think it sacrilegious
to have it off with a religious!
A heretic is not impressed
by any timid female dressed,
as Muslim wives are, in a shroud,
a heap of rags, and not allowed

to show her figure or her hair,
only her face exposed to air.
One would suspect that under all
those clothes as black as funeral pall,
what's there is better left unseen,
the pallid flesh too fat or lean
and hardly made for naughty play
after the whips are thrown away!

Ah, heretics! They miss the fun
of doing with a lovely nun
the very things forbidden in
the ten no-noes. A sense of sin
is the most zestful kind of spice
that makes the naughty deed so nice.
No Spanish fly, Viagra or
other enhancement could do more.

All this is voiced by Casanova
who's still an abbé, and moreover
one who attends each Sunday mass
(what if it's just to view his lass,
his piety is not in doubt –
in many ways he's quite devout!).
Man of his time, his deep convictions
are riddled through with contradictions.

And now the stately game begins
moving with all the outs and ins,
by which the female tests a male
before they start to close the sale –
the steamy hopes and icy fears
the gasps, the sighs, the burning tears,
until they reach the long delayed
hour when the *sacrifice* is made

to Venus *diva* with the graces
and loves, with many soft embraces
and words that set the heart on fire
as they accomplish their desire.
And that word *sacrifice*, we note,
is an expression which we quote
from Giacomo, who does not care
for coarse locutions anywhere.

Her face it is that wins his heart,
and half her forearm – no other part
is visible outside her habit.
Now to possess her he grows rabid,
if just to see her all unclothed.
He quite forgets his young betrothed,
goes with excitement to embrace
his new love in her special place,

a love-nest which her Frenchman rents –
and where she plays without pretence
her games outside the convent wall.
while telling her old lover all
she means to do with her Italian
– reportedly hung like a stallion,
and also learnèd and a wit.
The French envoy delights in it.

Like a man opening Christmas gifts
Giacomo parts her vests and shifts:
a bow undone at last discloses
her bosom, smelling sweet of roses,
and starting from their silken nests
perfection of her luscious breasts,
strawberry-tipped, of C-cup size,
such as bring tears to our man's eyes.

Sexual fantasy is kitsch
and all too often vulgar, which
prompts me to abdicate the thing
to readers' own imagining,
but keep it genial, in good taste,
and leisurely – no need for haste.
The partners, fanciful and strong
will play their games the whole night long.

While Giacomo is wildly playing
with Mary Magdalene and saying
many sweet nothings on the side,
someone is watching from a hide.
In fact, the French ambassador,
he's often viewed such scenes before,
and like a mouse behind the wainscot
he sees them *sacrifice* their brains out.

46

3.

Giacomo says: *Your place or mine?*
Our man has found a house so fine,
the rent so costly that he's mad
to think he can afford the pad!
Nevertheless he orders food –
oysters and truffles and other good
expensive nosh to fuel passion
while eagerly he waits to cash in!

The sanctum of this fane of Venus
reflects our Casanova's genius:
a room, octagonal in form,
where candelabra cast a warm
and golden light from all directions,
with mirror-glass repeats reflections
from walls and ceiling and the floor –
Narcissus could not ask for more!

And here our amorous divinity
repeats her beauties to infinity
with all her charms from every angle –
her hair a lovely auburn tangle
this way and that way in the galaxies
with candle-fires around the ecstasies
of lovers in the throes of Eros –
in truth a *sacrifice* for heroes!

Their images arrayed in ranks
display an infinite phalanx
seen here advance, and there retreat.
Her long limbs, tiny hands and feet
lit by the myriad candle-fires
ignite forever his desires,
forever in their love contend
in panorama without end.

Now all their body parts reflected,
by light dissected, then collected
as stars and flowers, form a vision
of geometrical precision
shifting their patterns with each move
of humans in the throes of love
what's up is down, what's down is up,
they're inside a kaleidoscope!

Amid the stars the lovers play
hither and over every way!
Miraculously multiplied
her lovely breasts from every side
fly off into the Milky Way,
she's Goddess of the latter day.
Our man will know no greater bliss
in all his many loves than this.

4.

Magdalene's charm is not just sexual,
she's also quite an intellectual
and fills her lover with delight
by talking classics half the night.
She loves to think and talk and joke
about Voltaire and Bolingbroke
and scorns the silly fairy-tales
priests blather from the altar rails.

Giacomo loves a girl with mind
who thinks, and thinking leaves behind
the superstitions of the past
and takes in new ideas fast.
Yet faced with one who *is* enlightened
he finds himself a little frightened.

His own free thought is a result
of alchemy and the occult.

His superstition is to treasure
a quite relentless cult of pleasure,
yet shares with his kind foster-father
a love of magic and a rather
irrational and curious fancy
for pseudo-faiths like necromancy,
though not against the law to hold
belief in turning lead to gold.

Their pillow-talk at times concerns
the labyrinthine twists and turns
of politics and civil jobbery,
and for the merchants licensed robbery.
Giacomo says the system works
and power's entitled to its perks;
self-interest drives the great machine,
hence the Republic's Most Serene.

As for the lady, what would *she* say
would work as a Venetian cliché
that could be, like, you know, made new?
And in the latest fashion too.
Something about the ship of state
built slightly crooked to go straight,
a gondola bent at the stern
to counter tendencies to turn.

Yet Giacomo is at his warmest
when feigning to be most conformist
and argues for the *status quo*
strongly and eloquently, though
in practice he's a happy rake,
a brilliant con-man on the make,
and still he strives to make his peace
with the Inquisitor's police.

So clever is young Magdalene
she likes to plan the games between
her lover and enlightened friends
and find new ways to gain their ends.
If pressed, she would at once confess
she does not think that more is less;
increase the numbers, so she holds,
and multiply the fun fourfold.

She hopes to heighten their affairs
by doubling up the amorous pairs
and first initiates the fun
by introducing two on one,
two girls, that is, with Casanova
over and over till it's over,
and then by way of an encore
to stage a bout with all the four!

Eros, exhausted, droops and hovers
above the tangled, busy lovers,
whose passion slowly ebbs, whereby
we learn the truth that love can die.
Too soon the envoy must depart,
breaking poor Magdalena's heart
and making Catarina pout
while Casanova feels left out.

Sea-fog shuts off the evening star,
makes far things near and near things far.
Above the haze on the lagoon
boatmen descry a watery moon.
Giacomo's eye is also wet
with what's for him a rare regret.
Remembering the apotheosis
of light-filled love, champagne and roses,

he sees how love is turned to ashes.
He wonders also where his cash is,
since thoughtlessly he's poured it out
– money well spent he'll never doubt –
but here he is without a sequin,
befogged, of poverty a-reeking,
a proud, conceited man struck down,
he'll be the butt of jokes in town.

He sees the Doge's gorgeous palace,
fancies it wears a frown of malice,
and looming from the fog a portent,
St Mark's looks like a sultan's war tent.
Our hero shudders. Over there,
huddled together in the square,
cloaked figures wearing mask and hat –
he has to wonder what they're at

for a few moments – oh but then!
Giacomo, cheerfulest of men,
from the canal hears violins,
sweet music to remit his sins
enhanced by distance, blown around
by the night breezes, with the sound
of flutes and lutes adrift in air,
now he's for bed without a care.

Never will young Catrin forget –
she'll wed a banker with regret;
and Magdalene, suppressing yearning,
will turn her brilliant mind to learning,
and after giving love this one vent
will end as abbess of the convent.
As for the envoy, priests will pardon all
his peccadilloes as a cardinal.

Ahead for Giacomo there lies
much of intrigue before he dies.
An English slut, with on- and offing,
will almost bring him to his coffin
(and thanks, Lord Byron, for the rhyme,
I'll pay you back another time),
her evil such, he cannot bear it
and at the last she breaks his spirit.

Masks and disguises

*The Women, Men, and persons of all Conditions disguising
themselves in antique dresses....*
                    – John Evelyn, 1646

At work Venetians can look stern,
they know they're well worth what they earn.
But at the ending of the day
they like to gussy up and play.
Masks are in order and illusion,
cross-dressing to create confusion,
a swaggering beau may be a belle,
and girls from men are hard to tell.

A nun in drag is quite amazing,
rose velvet coat with spangles blazing,
vest similar with golden stitches
above black taffeta silk breeches
fastened at knees with diamond buckles
to match the big ones on her knuckles.
Cocked hat and mask complete disguise –
you'd never tell her from the guys.

Giacomo loves to search her pockets
for golden chains and jewelled lockets,
two watches, sweet-box set with pearls,
kerchiefs of cambric soaked (for girls)
with perfume from a crystal vial,
enamelled snuff-box, latest style,
and last, what does his search reveal?
a pistol made of English steel!

Accoutred thus, she makes her way
with crowds from opera or play,
or hurrying on to take a chance
at cards, or even at romance,
and stops for coffee or for wine
before the hour she's set to dine,
after a change from fancy duds
with one or other of her studs.

Of Venice females all that we know
comes from the writer Aretino:
the work of wives is to raise progeny
while nuns and naughties try androgyny.
Rules of decorum can be less tight
for the well-bred, discreet transvestite;
the famed castrato's wildest fans
aren't sure he's not a courtesan.

Still, in the end we have to ask
why do Venetians love the mask?
Maybe because social routine –
dull rounds to see and to be seen
by the same persons, known too well –
is in its way a kind of hell.
Masked, who you are, no one need know;
be what you're not, your world will grow.

Another motive for disguise –
the swarms of Inquisition spies
reporting what you read and think,
how much you spend on girls or drink,
how often artisans contact
one who's an enemy in fact.
All foreigners you must avoid –
on this the council's paranoid.

From fifteen seven, Venice made
glass mirrors for the export trade
backed with bright mercury and tin
which soon secured a corner in
the market, holding it until
the secret leaked, as secrets will,
and Frenchmen crafted, by and by,
the Hall of Mirrors at Versailles.

Another point of anxious care
is silk production, an affair
involving many a secret skill
for which competitors would kill.
Sometimes these rivals in the trade
will mount a furtive talent raid,
and senators have jealous fits
and almost lose their fading wits.

To guard trade secrets is the charge
of council members, by and large,
for every foreign envoy tries
to infiltrate with clever spies
the workshops of the Veneto,
hence a strict law's enforced that no
Venetian may associate
with members of a rival state.

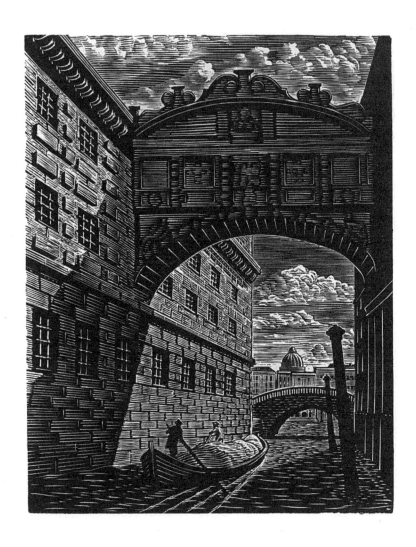

O City, city ...

There are grapes in the barges below, game of all kinds in the shops,
and vegetables laid out on the pavements.
— Pietro Aretino

O empire of the money-bag,
whose merchant rulers rake in swag,
where justice (that is not the word
which in plain speech should be preferred)
is in its action swift and silent
and terrible as it is violent;
even the Doge is not immune
when Counsellors don't like his tune,
and citizens awake dismayed
to see his severed head displayed.
Few of them ever will forget a
sight like this in the piazzetta.
To call this justice is an error,
these merchant-princes rule by terror;
it's cheaper than the fancy game
which other nations like to name
'fairness and equity', 'rule of law',
it costs far less to overawe
the people with a timely fright –
nor do they ask whether it's right.

Strangely the city they have made,
founded upon larcenous trade,
is of all earthly places best
in beauty, culture and the rest,
and what's more strange, her sea-empire
has lasted more or less entire
from here to Asia Minor's shore
a thousand years or even more.
For if her polity is tragic
her watery streets are simply magic.

Giacomo's spent a night of pain
losing his stakes twice and again
at a convenient gambling table
playing as long as he is able
with gold belonging to his darling –
by which of course this time I mean
the lovely Sister Magdalene –
and now is broke without a farthing.
(Forgive me for the lousy rhyme,
I'll try to better it next time.)

As dawn begins to stain the sky
with gold, then green and burning rose,
our man with other losers goes
across the Grand Canal, while standing
in a gondola, to a landing
near the arcaded Pescheria
and the adjacent Erberia.
Here revellers may calm their nerves
with sight of things that nature serves
to show a vegetable diet
(hold on – don't knock it till you try it);
there's sanity in cauliflowers
while lettuce soothes the troubled hours,
and beans do more than Latin psalms
to fill the beggar's cup with alms.

Here to this glimmering canal
come wide rafts, barges, laden all
with produce from the isles nearby
which, with the mainland farms, supply
the markets of the waking town.

See the potatoes, gold and brown,
yellow and green the piled zucchini
next to the purple melanzane,
mushrooms and funghi from the woods.
Come, look on Ceres' teeming goods
all shining with an inner light
(Elizabeth David gets that right)
which calms and soothes the agitation
of a neurotic generation.

And that, dear friends, is just the effect
of chlorophyll on intellect.
Think what the force of flowers must be
when they're arranged for all to see!
The fragile faces of the blooms
can of themselves disperse the glooms.
The sweetest blossoms of July,
all on display to please the eye,
bring solace to the weary thought
of the pained soul who's overwrought.
So, homeward now – jiggety-jigs!
Giacomo goes back to his digs –
to find the lodging in uproar –
who could have smashed his bedroom door?

The red, enraged landlady knew:
the Inquisition's thugs, that's who!
Searching, they made her understand,
for a locked trunk of contraband.

What did the locked trunk contain?
Just salt, they say, but they maintain
no excise duty has been paid.
A poor excuse for such a raid.
Stunned by the dazzle of the morning
our man does not perceive the warning.
Friends look on him with sudden pity:
For your own safety, flee the city!
Get out of town, don't hesitate –
An hour from now may be too late!

The great ordeal

Quem deus vult perdere prius dementat.

His friends insist he has been warned –
such fears, he thinks, should just be scorned.
Invulnerable, he's too clever
to be a tribune's victim ever.
Grateful, of course, he's touched to learn
the measure of his friends' concern.
Whom the gods frog-march to the pits,
first they deprive him of his wits.

Giacomo thinks their fears unfounded
and all in foolish rumour grounded;
he's not aware of any crime
that he's committed – for some time.
Since he's without a sense of guilt
he'll prove his virtue to the hilt.
Inquisitors must understand,
he's not involved in contraband.

For after all, where is the harm
in yielding to a woman's charm?
How can it possibly be crime
to seek one's pleasure all the time?
And how could anyone arrive at
the notion that what's thought in private
could ever hurt or give offence
to anyone with common sense?

His kindly patron pleads in vain –
To stay in Venice is insane!
Leave now, avoid the tribune's malice,
or shelter briefly in my palace.
Authority will hesitate
before it dares to violate
a noble's house. But best begone!

Take flight for Mestre and beyond!

Giacomo tries to calm these fears,
abandoning his friend to tears.
His patron says, with looks of pain,
I fear we'll never meet again.
(And meet again they never would –
this is the day they part for good.)
Giacomo is fatigued and mindless;
there's no accounting for his blindness.

At last at home in bed again
he sleeps with all his might and main.
Of dreams he'll have no recollection,
nor of matutinal erection,
but fully conscious at first light
he wakes untimely in a fright –
someone is standing by the door
tapping his boot upon the floor.

Giacomo feels a sudden freeze –
it's Messer-Grande, chief of police,
a brute known for his cruelty:
the monster calls out *Come with me,
if Casanova is your name!*
Our hero answers *I'm that same.*
When asked by what authority,
The Tribunal! says Messer-G.

Hearing this word, our Casanova,
conceding that the game is over,
is numb and dumb and deep in shock,
and still that way when under lock
and key within the Doge's jail,
where all but stoutest hearts must quail,
high up beneath the roofing lead.
He feels he is already dead.

Sweet liberty

I shall not die but shall declare the works of the Lord.

Consider now those nation-states
where merchants rule, and commerce rates
more highly than the public good
(the rulers hate the multitude),
where truth and equity and justice
are left to putrefy and rust as
far too costly to afford,
while force and money are adored.

Venice will join in a Crusade –
but only if she's richly paid.
Meanwhile her navy's up for rent
at cost plus twenty-five percent,
and at the end the spoils of war
show glittering in her churches, or
bring grandeur to her public spaces
and the façades of noble places.

The city, huddled in its islands,
some of it swamps and elsewhere dry lands.
brings all its treasures to the fore –
windows of a department store –
and sometimes what we think is beauty,
the spectacle of so much booty
won by the mercenary sword,
can look more like a robber's hoard.

In such a state where business reigns,
the only value lies in *gains*.
Conscience is cleansed with other soap
by priest and patriarch and pope,
who in return demand control
of every living Christian soul –
and what of Justice? Well, what *of* it?

Due process never showed a profit.

So what's the charge? There's no such thing,
it costs the state too much to bring
a wretch to trial, with the expense
of testing all the evidence.
As for the sentence, there's no need
to tell the prisoner, or heed
his fear of facing the garotte.
Throw him in jail and let him rot!

Giacomo feels the heavy weight
Of the displeasure of the state,
but then – I've never known it fail –
like any other wretch in jail,
pleads innocence of any crime
at this or any other time.
It's a mistake, they'll let him out,
and *soon*, he entertains no doubt.

Creatures whose lives are wild and free
when brought into captivity,
restrained and caged, their space confined,
sicken and pine away. Their kind
cannot be tamed or taught to live
in cages, and do not survive
efforts to help them through the day,
but quickly die when locked away.

It's true some birds don't seem to mind
the well-fed life of the confined,
and from their narrow cages sing
tunes that declare Let Freedom ring!
But if you set them free to fly
they'll wing their way into the sky.

In Buddhist temples, you may pay
to let the captives fly away.

With humankind, the average bloke
will bow his neck to bear the yoke
and tread the same path, shine or rain,
from home to work and back again.
Challenged to take a risky shot
at liberty – he'd rather not,
unlike the truly noble soul
who cannot tolerate control.

Such is our Giacomo, a chap
for whom commitment is a trap –
even in love, he still feels free
to fool around with two or three.
And promises! – he'll quickly make 'em
and later just as quickly break 'em.
These are the ways of Freedom's son –
he's looking out for Number One!

He enters by the Bridge of Sighs
and, coming to his cell, he spies
with horror, fastened to the wall,
a grim device that would appal
the stoutest heart to come upon.
Its use is to do justice on
persons condemned to strangulation
at the Tribunal's instigation.

Next thing, he's locked up in the Leads,
a fate that every captive dreads,
in garrets underneath the roof,
reputed to be breakout-proof,
where filthy rats and fleas at play
torment the prisoners every day.
Summer dismays with heat and thirst,
but winter's icy chills are worst.

Giacomo suffers, shocked and numb,
there's not a chance that help will come;
the cell too low for him to stand,
the walls too close on either hand.
His vital force begins to fail –
he fears he'll not survive in jail.
Then fever strikes, to burn his brain
and torture him with weeks of pain.

A doctor comes to purge and bleed;
he warns Giacomo to take heed
and not succumb to melancholy –
to die of sorrow would be folly.
Aroused, the patient turns depression
into blind rage that breeds aggression.
They mean to keep him here forever?
Well, he can break out if he's clever!

As when the eagle, soaring high,
scans the wide plain with searching eye,
sees and locks onto living prey
and every sense comes into play
focused upon the dive and strike,
so Giacomo, intent alike
on one sole end, looks for a nail
or any tool to break from jail.

And finds at last an iron rod
which, sharpened, makes a spike to prod
between the bricks and leads – also
to serve as pike for thrust or blow.
should the escaper be attacked.
Though honing it requires, in fact,
many long days of toil and stress,
here time's one asset in excess.

And so for many days ahead
Giacomo digs beneath his bed;
on the last night he'll break right through
to the secretary's office below
and slither down a linen rope
of bedsheets, which will hold, we hope.
until he gains the floor below.
From there to freedom he will go.

So much for plans. Yet on the day
before the night to break away,
his jailer has good news to tell –
he's to be moved to a big cell
with windows and good ventilation!
Disaster, horror, consternation!
Out of the frying-pan to the fire!
So read it all in his *Memoir*.

It's not our job to steal his glory
by telling once again the story
on which he dined out all his days.
Ours but to comment and to praise
a tale of daring far to seek,
in human fantasy unique.
Our hero's hopes are crushed for now,
but look, he will survive the row.

Casanova's Rod

My bar thus sharpened formed an eight-sided dagger, and
would have done justice to a first-rate cutler.... It was
dear to me as the instrument of freedom, and was worthy of
being hung as an ex voto on the altar of liberty.

Arthur, Cu, Scarface, move over,
make room for hero Casanova!
each with his warrior's attribute,
a sword to cut, a gun to shoot,
(and for the Gael a thing more vulgar,
a secret weapon called *gae bulga*).
Excalibur is Arthur's blade,
Scarface's gun is Yankee-made.

And Giacomo's to stab and pierce
is a pike useful and most fierce!
Heaven hurled a bolt into Earth's crust
and there it slept in rock and rust
until Hephaestus drained its iron
by turning a volcano's fire on
then cooled and in the ocean tempered
the ingot till it's banged and hammered

to forge a supernatural spike
of which no man has seen the like.
Let its diameter be *x*,
(roughly as thick as a male sex
organ) 'x-calibre' its name.
Excalibur II for lasting fame!
For in this weapon fire resides,
with water, air and earth besides.

With this, if needs be, he will kill
any man who would thwart his will,
and yet he keeps a strict control
on passions raging in his soul.
In the event, while he succeeds
in all his conflicts, no one bleeds,
except himself when squeezing by
a splintered door which rips each thigh.

Apotheosis

*My pike is an admirable instrument, but I can make no
use of it since my cell is sounded all over (except the
ceiling) every day. If I would escape it is by the ceiling,
therefore, that way I must go, but to do that I must
make a hole through it, and that I cannot do from my
side, for it would not be the work of a day. I must have
someone to help me....*

Love has been Giacomo's school,
its strategy his guiding rule;
though never did he see before
how very close love is to war,
and is in many ways the same,
each being a planned strategy game;
one's moves in both adjusted to
what the antagonist may do.

First principle is choose the aim,
then keep on it throughout the game.
Giacomo's first attempt is foiled,
the larger thrust survives unspoiled.
New tactics will be difficult
but, aimed at similar result,
can still succeed if he persists
through fortune's many turns and twists.

The aim is simple – Liberty
(and, bear in mind, simplicity
in all of military lore
is also a first rule of war).
This time, our hero has to own,
there's no way he can act alone;
he needs a trusted partner to
help him in what he has to do.

A troop of two? It would be grand
if Casanova could command
and if the other could obey –
while out of sight, too, by the way.
First step, to plan the operation,
is, institute communication
with prisoners in the next-door cell
and this he manages so well,

that in good time he has control
of a next-door captive's soul.
and now thinks out a daring plan
that utilizes this new man.
But can he be depended on
in this hard operation?
Trust this – whatever shall be shall be,
the only hope is Father Balbi.

This Balbi's noble and a monk,
a womanizer and a drunk,
the fellow's pretty stupid too,
but hey! what is a man to do?
One uses means that are to hand
and hopes the fool will understand.
So, stupid, read me carefully.
Obey my orders – and be free.

Pause for a moment, contemplate
the truly mad and desperate
ordeal that these men confront.
First the escape and then the hunt
as all the force of law and order
pursues them to the nation's border.
But first, break out! And then to scale
the roof, where death strikes if they fail!

Like the commander of a great
army, who must communicate,
in writing, every scheme and plan,
our hero drives his single man
by written messages in code
or rather Latin of church mode,
and such the force of our man's soul,
the monk obeys them, sole and whole.

The moon is down, and dark the air,
astride the rooftop two men stare,
free of their walls and prison bars,
into the night-sky's swarm of stars.
Above them glows the universe,
the stars recalled from Dante's verse,
the glimmering fires of liberty –
still pain will come before they're free.

St Mark's domes huddle dark ahead,
grey like the roofs with tiles of lead,
and on the left the tower looms
of the tall campanile. The glooms
of sleeping houses on the right
show here and there a gleam of light;
gondolas nodding at their tether
like restive horses crowd together.

The drowsy oarsmen in their bark,
ready for custom though it's dark,
drink grappa to clear out their throats
and loudly hail the passing boats
and slap their shoulders with their arms
believing action wakes and warms.
Only such fellows of the night
are waking or will show a light.

And all around the world's asleep
except a few supposed to keep
their vigil, and to warn of fire.
The Doge snores in his rich attire,
fine linen nightcap and the best
of bedclothes to assure his rest.
About him all the courtiers lie
exhausted by their industry.

Commercial nobles above shops
sleep with the aid of opium drops,
or doped with wines of Veneto
struggle and snore both loud and low;
the executioners have dreams
of tortured malefactors' screams,
and wreathed in smiles repose their heads
on goosedown in their feather-beds.

Behind their shutters workers lie
tossing and turning with a sigh;
they sleep, the sane and lunatics,
the saintly souls and heretics.
The Patriarch, whose bladder's weak,
rises for a nocturnal leak,
somnambulist, he leaves his cot
and reaches for the chamber-pot.

While Casanova lifts his eyes
to the vast cupola of skies
where great beasts of the Zodiac
pursue their everlasting track.
Also the Great Bear soars aslant
and armed Orion makes his hunt
through the black labyrinth of space;
his own sign of the Ram he'll trace.

His glistening eye reflects the far light,
the myriad fires of distant starlight
and faint and far upon his ears
steals the grand music of the spheres;
which light and sound dissolve his soul
and draw it to its heavenly goal.
His zombie body plods meanwhile
to earthly freedom and exile.

Deep in his mind – he has to know it –
he knows his blessing as a poet;
the worst disaster that befell him
could still, despite his anguish, tell him
a truth about our human plight
and in our darkness show a light –
and at the last a broken heart
by poetry transmutes to art.

And see, the dismal tiles of lead
are turned to shining gold instead!
The dreadful memory recalled
new generations read, appalled
to see misfortunes turned to farces
and generate a strange catharsis.
This is the poet's famous stone –
some say it comes from God alone.

Look for Giacomo in the sky,
lover of girls and liberty,
for censure he won't give a damn
now he's ensconced beside the Ram.
Forever laughing, always young,
his vital spirit lives among
the prettiest women everywhere;
with every one of them he'll share

his potent charm in bed and board.
Now he's a myth, he can afford
to enter lives denied in life,
bring joy to a neglected wife,
or make a timid maiden brave
enough to do the thing she'd crave,
and find that, after all, it's nice
to spend her nights in sacrifice.

Listen to what the Muses sing,
nothing is lost – or everything!
Our words, for better or for worse,
resound throughout the universe;
O hark! that whispering solar wind
could be dim echoes of the sound
of the Big Bang from which began
events that bred Eve and her man.

Explicit Liber Casanovae

About Kildare Dobbs

Kildare Dobbs is an award-winning writer and poet who has lived
the world over. Born in 1923, in India, Dobbs was raised in
Ireland, and educated in Dublin, Cambridge and London. After
serving in the Royal Navy during World War II and in East
Africa, Dobbs finally migrated to Canada in 1952 and worked in
journalism and publishing. His autobiography, *Running to Paradise*
(1962), won a Governor-General's Award, and since then he has
published various collections of short stories, novellas and poetry,
including *The Great Fur Opera* (1970). In 2000, he was invested
with the Order of Ontario, and installed as Writer-in-Residence
at the University of Toronto in 2002. His memoir, *Running the
Rapids,* was published in 2005. Kildare Dobbs now lives and writes
in Toronto.